W9-BZP-883

WITHDRAWN

PHOENIXVILLE PUBLIC LIBRARY
183 SECOND AVENUE
PHOENIXVILLE, PA 19460-3843

WITHDRAWN

No Backbone!
The World of Invertebrates

Slimy Sea Slugs

by Natalie Lunis

Consultant: Bill Murphy
Marine Biologist, Northern Waters Gallery
New England Aquarium
Boston, MA

BEARPORT
PUBLISHING

NEW YORK, NEW YORK

Credits

Cover and TOC, © Marianne Bones/Shutterstock and © Daniel Gustavsson/Shutterstock; Title Page, © Daniel Gustavsson/Shutterstock; 4T, © Cheryl A. Meyer/Shutterstock; 4B, © Georgette Douwma/naturepl.com; 5, © Phillip Colla/SeaPics.com; 6, © Mike Wilkes/npl/Minden Pictures; 7, © Jeff Jaskolski/SeaPics.com; 9, © Doug Perrine/SeaPics.com; 10T, © Michael & Patricia Fogden/Minden Pictures; 10B, © John Cancalosi/naturepl.com; 11, © John C. Lewis/SeaPics.com; 12, © Carol Buchanan/Alamy; 13, © Zigmund Leszczynski/Animals Animals Earth Scenes; 14T, © James D. Watt/SeaPics.com; 14B, © Peter Parks/iq3-d/SeaPics.com; 15, © Mark Strickland/SeaPics.com; 17, © Marc Chamberlain/SeaPics.com; 19, © Roger Steene/imagequestmarine.com; 20T, © W. Gregory Brown/Animals Animals Earth Scenes; 20M, © Brandon D. Cole/CORBIS; 20B, © Jez Tryner/SeaPics.com; 21, © Clay Wiseman/Animals Animals Earth Scenes; 22TL, © David Schrichte/SeaPics.com; 22TR, © age fotostock/SuperStock; 22BL, © Hans Leijnse/FOTO NATURA/Minden Pictures; 22BR, © Marc Chamberlain/SeaPics.com; 22 Spot, © Asther Lau Choon Siew/Shutterstock; 23TL, © Jim Wehtje/Photodisc Green/Getty Images; 23TR, © Daniel Gustavsson/Shutterstock; 23BL, © Peter Parks/iq3-d/SeaPics.com; 23BR, © Marc Chamberlain/SeaPics.com.

Publisher: Kenn Goin
Editorial Director: Adam Siegel
Creative Director: Spencer Brinker
Design: Dawn Beard Creative
Photo Researcher: Nancy Tobin

Library of Congress Cataloging-in-Publication Data

Lunis, Natalie.
  Slimy sea slugs / by Natalie Lunis.
      p. cm. — (No backbone! The world of invertebrates)
  Includes bibliographical references and index.
  ISBN-13: 978-1-59716-511-2 (library binding)
  ISBN-10: 1-59716-511-5 (library binding)
  1. Nudibranchia—Juvenile literature. I. Title.

  QL430.4.L86 2008
  594'.36—dc22

                         2007014798

Copyright © 2008 Bearport Publishing Company, Inc. All rights reserved. No part of this publication may be reproduced in whole or in part, stored in any retrieval system, or transmitted in any form or by any means, electronic, mechanical, photocopying, recording, or otherwise, without written permission from the publisher.

For more information, write to Bearport Publishing Company, Inc., 101 Fifth Avenue, Suite 6R, New York, New York 10003. Printed in the United States of America.

10 9 8 7 6 5 4 3 2 1

Contents

Slugs of the Sea

Sea slugs are animals that live in the sea.

Like land slugs, they are just snails without shells.

They are also animals without **backbones**.

In fact, slugs and snails don't have any bones at all in their soft bodies.

Many kinds of slugs and snails live on land. Even more kinds live in the ocean.

land slug

snail

Trails of Slime

Land slugs make trails of slime with their bodies.

The slime helps them move along the ground.

Sea slugs make trails of slime, too.

The slime helps them move along the ocean floor.

Many sea slugs have feathery **gills** on their backs. The gills help them breathe underwater.

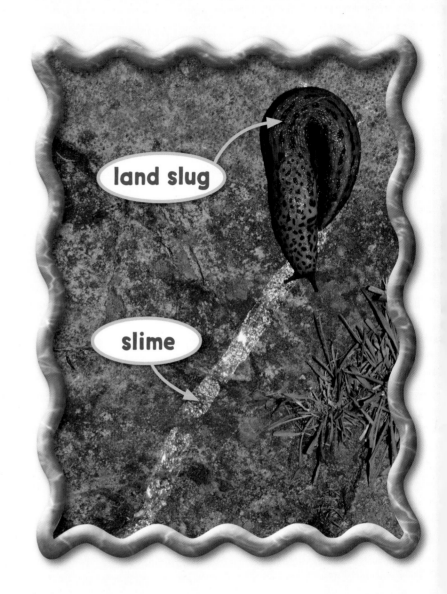

land slug

slime

Protected by Poison

Snails have shells that protect their soft bodies.

Sea slugs don't.

They have other ways to stay safe from enemies.

Many kinds of slugs are full of poison.

The poison can make other animals sick.

Some sea slugs can make a special kind of slime that has poison in it.

Warning Colors

Animals that are poisonous are often brightly colored.

Many kinds of sea slugs are very colorful.

The reds, yellows, oranges, and purples on their soft bodies warn other animals to back off.

Some brightly colored sea slugs are not poisonous. Their bright colors fool enemies and keep them away.

poisonous frog

poisonous snake

Almost No Enemies

Not all sea slugs use color to stand out.

Some use it to blend in.

They can hide on sand or among rocks and plants.

Other sea slugs give off a bad smell.

With so many ways to protect themselves, sea slugs have almost no enemies.

sea spider

Sea spiders are one of the few animals that eat sea slugs.

sea slug

13

Meat Eaters

Land slugs eat plants, but sea slugs eat mainly other animals.

Most sea slugs move very slowly, however.

They can only catch animals that are even slower.

Often they eat sponges, corals, and other animals that don't move at all.

Some sea slugs are good swimmers. They catch **plankton** and other small creatures that swim.

sponge

plankton

sea slug

coral

15

Follow That Trail

Some sea slugs use their sense of smell to hunt.

They follow the trails of slime that other slugs leave behind.

Then they catch and eat the slugs.

Sea slugs have two pairs of **tentacles**. One pair can smell food. The other pair can feel things.

Poison for Dinner

Sometimes sea slugs eat jellyfish and other animals that have poison of their own.

The poison does not hurt the sea slugs, though.

Instead, it is stored in their own bodies.

It helps protect the sea slugs from being eaten themselves!

Sea slugs sometimes get their color from the animals they eat. Some eat orange sponges and turn orange. Others eat yellow sponges and turn yellow.

sea slug eating
Pacific man-of-war

19

Colorful Names

There are about 3,000 kinds of sea slugs.

They live in all the world's oceans.

Sea slugs are some of the most colorful animals on Earth.

People have given them some very interesting names to tell about their colorful bodies.

The most colorful sea slugs live in places where the ocean is warm.

lettuce sea slug

orange peel sea slug

fried egg sea slug

blueberry
sea slug

21

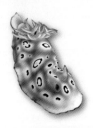

A World of Invertebrates

Animals that have backbones are known as *vertebrates* (VUR-tuh-brits). Mammals, birds, fish, reptiles, and amphibians are all vertebrates.

Animals that don't have backbones are *invertebrates* (in-VUR-tuh-brits). Worms, jellyfish, squids, and sea slugs are all invertebrates. So are all insects and spiders. More than 95 percent of all kinds of animals are invertebrates.

Here are four invertebrates that are related to sea slugs. Like sea slugs, they all live in the ocean.

Abalone

Periwinkles

Whelk

Conch

Glossary

backbones
(BAK-*bohnz*)
a group of
connected bones
that run along
the backs of some
animals, such as
dogs, cats, and fish;
also called spines

gills (GILZ)
body parts
that help sea
slugs breathe
underwater

plankton
(PLANGK-tuhn)
tiny animals and
plants that float in
oceans and lakes

tentacles
(TEN-tuh-kuhlz)
body parts that
help sea slugs
smell food and
feel things

Index

Read More

Kite, Patricia.
Down in the Sea: The Sea Slug. Morton Grove, IL: Albert Whitman & Company (1994).

Tesar, Jenny.
What on Earth Is a Nudibranch? Woodbridge, CT: Blackbirch Press (1995).

Weber, Valerie J.
Sea Slugs. Milwaukee, WI: Gareth Stevens Publishing (2005).

Learn More Online

To learn more about sea slugs, visit **www.bearportpublishing.com/NoBackbone**